The Train To Sunshine

Sarah Hafeez

BookLeaf Publishing

India | USA | UK

Dedication

To the magic of the written word

Preface

Through this collection of poems, I have endeavored to evoke fragments of thoughts, both imagined and reflective, and of experiences lived. The verses are mostly conversational in style and the themes diverse. I trust that the voices, images, emotions, thoughts, and feelings encapsulated in these poems will resonate with you, the reader.

Acknowledgements

In heartfelt gratitude to my families, for their constant love and support; my teachers, for being the driving force behind my pursuit of knowledge; and my friends, for being my first readers.

1. hometown blues

is there a name
for tell-tale turmeric-stained hunger
in the alleyways of small-town hearts,

where childhood took leaps of faith
into plunging depths of blue dreams,

where trains of upper-class haughtiness
trundled past waving fields of poor envy,

where avuncular advice was bestowed
with priestly prominence
and paternal decrees determined destinies,

where love blossomed in shy lily-laced sightings
on country-side bicycle-rides,

where the moon looked more magical than fireflies
on dark heart-broken nights,

where the news of a confirmed city government-post
brought tears, of pride, to motherly eyes,

as it did, of impending separation,
in me?

2. spiced rice

biryani aromas fill me
with my mother's love,
flavoured with condiments
of imposed table manners
and imaginings of an Indian *nawab*
deported to distant lands
with their rice-potato
and cattle-women –
sunshine on my plate,
my *dastarkhwan* is a battlefield,
serving the eternal question of supremacy –
Hyderabadi, Kolkata, Awadhi, Veg?

~

raita asides – Does the *garam-masala*
of eternal, lonely kitchen labour
singe mothers' hearts,
while fathers go to fend for family?

3. guru dakshina

calloused, soiled hands
gently guide clean, soft young fingers
to the spinning mound of mud.

fascinated, impressionable soil
is softly, over time, moulded into
an article of beauty –

it takes the shape of both
the masterful strokes of experience
and the freshness of new direction.

~

I am the
sum of all my teachers –
my learning is my only capital.

4. fabricated fragrances

I sift through
freshly watered garden roses
and pick the
sweetest-smelling flowers,
before traffic soot
envelopes their beauty
in merciless onslaught.

as I arrange the flowers
in coloured buckets
on this wintry pavement morning,
elder brother calls me,
for the first time
since I moved to the big city,
asking what I have been up to.

I lie —
I am beating
an iron pan flat,
and welding a

broken pot anew
in the ironsmith's apprenticeship.

even as I speak to him,
I think —
do I deceive because I fear
loss of face?
will I be able to bear the taunts
of my village folk
who consider girlish flowers
a waste?

the conversation comes to a close,
finally.
I put down the phone,
and am lost in thought
about being found out,
when I notice that
the roses I had picked
have begun wilting.

5. musty memories

afternoon office ennui
resurrects sepia snapshots
from an album called childhood.
~
I accuse the help
of being a thief when I lose a toy
and childhood innocence.
I flee in fear of
a school senior
threatening to report me.
I donate (finally) all my
abandoned jeans and t-shirts
to embrace ethnic wear.
I wear the only black dress
I will ever have,
on a stolen trial room-evening.
I harbour faith before I am
de-God-ed by learned red books,
And unread the same red books
when I am lost.

~

The rustle of paper
and the tinkle of screens going blank
un-anchor my thoughts –
I begin packing up to go home.

~

is growing up
an ageing museum?

are visitors allowed?

6. nuance

tomorrow I will become a language –

either cradled in a mother's lullaby,

or shapeless in a young lover's clumsy appeal,

akin to water stored in compliments and curses alike,

or lending colour to the itinerant caravan's tale,

or gathering dust in a grammarian's directory,

or locked in pure combat with a rival tongue,

or will I be sweet like Parsi sugar

dissolved in a glass brimming with national milk?

7. writer's block

my ode to the blank page
is a blank page –
it takes me nowhere,
yet, it is pregnant with possibilities – through it
I can afford to sail to
fragrant evenings of distant lands
or mete unjust justice to a young miscreant
in the black alleyways of a white city,
I can waltz with my lover's final adieu
on a rainy sunset
or announce national decrees to
teach the other a lesson,
I can apologize for
a snuffed-out people centuries later
or studiously analyze the reality of
remote villages of hunger-death,
I can erase identifies off maps
or erase maps off the world,
I can promise hope to
the passionate pen

of the unlettered girl,
I can breathe life into
curses and dreams alike,
I can, I can.

8. error 404: not found

the crescent of my eye lash
delicately perched on the universe of
an afternoon cup of tea
finally gets me thinking about reaching out

~

hello,
would you know of a help who
can wash away 12 pm ennui
from punishing eternity of
'the groceries amount to...'
or
one who can dust away the pain
of tea-time silences,
who can sweep and tuck away
signs of my absent children
or
tidy up shelves
still clutching onto
long-unfitting clothes.
can they make

a phone call or two
to lost friends
or draw blinds
over peeking windows?
can they mend
old wounds
from irreparable relationships
or,
at least, fix a tear or two?
can they rehome me?

9. scheming, plotting

shadowed by brick walls
flower buds begin to wilt –
a new housing scheme

~

where every leaf is a heartbeat
showered with the symphony of sun-rain love,
they dream to be a tree someday
touching skies unending,
nurturing a world –
creatures big and small, all sheltered and fed
by nature's most exquisite form of poetry.

~

the plot to cut trees
advertised with promise of
green acres of life

10. bustle

the poetry is in my city –
its soiled footprints
mapping immigrant hopes,
its traffic woes and
hot unworking-afternoons,
its exhausted sunset
heading to the inviting tavern,
its parrot-card reader
making money off our fears,
its destiny-less men
shouldering promethean weights,
its fierce women eking a living
scrubbing rich homes clean,
its sweaty brothel nights
teaming with insects,
its last trees
kissing the earth,
its concrete condominium-ed curse
sprouting everywhere,
its jeans-sporting love blossoming

on prying park-benches,
its street-children
weathering merciless storms,
its orders and petitions
waltzing years away in an unjust dance –
its pain, its suffering, its weeping,
its joys, its pleasures, its dreams and desires –
my city is a caravan.
it shelters a world.

11. telephonically speaking

my loves are singing the blues –
through the telephone screen.
my mother calls me every night
and asks after my diet,
my husband messages me his
'How is everything' from office-fed distances,
my brother, from another country,
sends me photos of his new flat-on-rent,
my friend forwards a voice note
describing her recent lion safari,
my father emails me his latest article
on the 3-year-war,
my niece video-calls me every week
to showcase her sketching skills –
in constant touch, I do not feel that alone –
but I miss my mother's hug,
the paternal pat on my head,
my husband's tea-time chatter,
friendly college-time banter,
the brotherly warmth of a meal prepared,

the endless happy hours of doctor-nurse games.

~

can the screen connect me
to those embroidered,
felt moments of togetherness?

12. insta-ready

all my rough work
is delicately, carefully
tucked
in the rear pages
of my star-spangled notebook –
so that
I appear as flawless
on the front pages of life,
as I do
on my social media wall.
picture-perfect,
my smile is copy-pasted
to endless reams
for others to read,
while my struggles
with life's miscalculations
only begin at the end.

13. customer satisfaction

I place a sliver of sacrifice,
a pint of care,
a hug or two, here and there,
into my cart.
let me see, what else –
ah,
a 1-liter bottle of compromise
and a packet of adjustment,
a slice of promises to be kept,
a whole bundle of time together,
a one and half-pound loaf of understanding
and a vial of mind-reading
need to go in as well,
and then of course,
a giant leap of faith.

~

at check-out, I am already eager
for discounts and cashbacks,
carefully reading the fine print
in return and refund policies.

Congratulations!
You have successfully placed your order for Love.

14. hazed identity

if images are fake
and reality alternate,
if double-speak the norm
blaring from world microphones,
if lies and morphed truths
are sponsored editorial policies,
if algorithms are listening in
on the inner workings of our minds,
and computer screens displaying
our deepest desires and fears alike,
then am I living in a sci-fi movie,
or am I a character in a horror novel,
am I a dystopian figment
of a poet's imagination,
or just a numerical code
written into a computer program?
who am I?

15. evening chants

sacred

is the heaven
in my mother's feet

a father teaching
his toddler to pray

the stars cooling
the embers of the bygone day

the oil lamp alight
at the foot of a towering tree

the *muezzin*'s call at dusk
chiming with temple and church bells

the wrinkled hope in
a homeless woman's appeal

the myna chirping at my window
on an early spring morn

the blanketed pup
on a wintry pavement

a flower blossoming
from among sand grains

the eye painted on
the embarking goddess adorned

the paper boat set afloat
in childlike delight

the first monsoon showers
leaving surprised lovers drenched,

sacred
is all that is truth, beauty.

16. eclipsed

every day:
I try masking my skin
in a c of vitamin
and mineral extracts
for a glowing strobe-like persona.
I try coating it in *Multani* mud packs
to tone away wrinkles and cracks
with the brush stroke
of white-moisturizer ads.
I desperately try erasing pimples and acne
and even a mole here and there
to look star-dust bright
in the night sky of 'beauty standards'.
I even choose my bathing soap
to make me cope
with tears of greasy, stubbornly
inherited colour.

17. chess board

late afternoon in my mother's heart
is a tapestry of inherited silences
and sanguine dreamless nights
checkered with the homely tussles
of an ancient, defeated queen.
her secret files of unfulfilled dreams –
a driver's license,
an Urdu diploma course,
a sports-day certificate of participation –
are carefully tucked away under ageing sarees.

~

her singing voice, a hidden jewel,
is set on permanent privacy settings –
raspy now, with feeble authority,
it tries conjuring that maternal right
over our lives,
while we adamantly overrule –
we are only guests in your *sarai*,
stopping over for a cup of tea or two
and some noon-time chatter.

18. reconstruction

if tomorrow
the sky is no longer blue
and home a vestige of
a number in my directory,
if you are decades away from me
with my heart wallowing in pangs of guilt,
if my name becomes a map of your lost poesy
and my love a forecast of inclement indecisions,
if my heart is caged in the ruins of miscalculations
and your lifetime worth of affection lies wasted
on the sanguine seat of sunset,
is there hope for us still
to pick shards of shattered words and voices
writ loud on the silent pages of separation,
and build back something new?

19. mother's shirt

mother's ivory-hued shirt,
a gift, is still crisp from the 1990 rains —

tried on once before the mirror
and she too embarassed to walk out
in it before my father or anyone else,

it smells of her jasmine itar
that has conquered the cupboard
despite its drawered incarceration.

when she passes it down to me today,
I reject is as too loose and old-fashioned,
I am jeans-thick skinned — I do not wear shirts.

so, her shroud-like attire is once more
embalmed in its 43-year-old casket,
and her grief-stained oft-worn dupattas —

they offer their condolences and hide

the pain behind the veil of
a living woman's dead desires.

20. waterless

where will I turn to when water
will no longer be my language of pain
or bathe the darling buds of spring in maternal rain?

where will I turn to when water
will turn neon from industrial pollution
and contaminate my prayer-time ablutions?

where will I turn to when water
will no longer reflect the skies aflutter
and, instead, snake through black city gutters?

where will I turn to when water
will no longer soften forest soil
or quench arid fields of hopeless toil?

where will I turn to when water
is no more, to bid adieu to the last breath
awaiting release in prelude to inevitable death?

where will I turn to,
oh, where?

21. bird song

there is inescapable joy
in typing '*termeric*',
and then pressing backspace
to correct the first 'e' to the 'u'.
there is ecstasy in fleshing out
the rhyme in poetic meter,
with 'packs' matching 'cracks',
and 'skin' akin to 'vitamin'.
there is enchanting joy in
negating capital punishment
meted out to sentence-openers,
and, instead, freeing the alphabet
from syntactical bondages.
~

love for the clickety-clack
of a musical keyboard
can keep me occupied
for infinite hours,
as I sit immersed in pilgrimage
to poesy.

www.ingramcontent.com/pod-product-compliance
Lightning Source LLC
Chambersburg PA
CBHW071235140726
47996CB00007B/2613